Corporal and Spiritual

WORKS OF MERCY

How God's Love Transforms Your Heart

Helping You Bring the Joy of the Faith to Your Family

Truly, I say to you, as you did it to one of the least
of these My brethren, you did it to Me.

Matthew 25:40

Author: **Kenneth L. Davison, Jr.**   Illustrations: **Caroline Spinelli and Chris Peliçano**

Excerpts from the Revised Standard Version of the Bible, 2nd edition, ©1971 by the Division of Christian Education of the National Council of the Churches of Christ in the United States of America. Used by permission. All rights reserved. Some Scripture texts in this work are taken from the *New American Bible*, revised edition©2010, 1991, 1986, 1970 Confraternity of Christian Doctrine, Washington, D.C. and are used by permission of the copyright owner. All Rights Reserved. No part of the *New American Bible* may be reproduced in any form without permission in writing from the copyright owner.

Excerpts from the English translation of *The Roman Missal* ©2010, International Commission on English in the Liturgy Corporation. All rights reserved.

Excerpts from the English translation of the *Catechism of the Catholic Church* for use in the United States of America Copyright ©1994, United States Catholic Conference, Inc.—Libreria Editrice Vaticana. Used with Permission.

DEDICATION

This book is dedicated to two modern saints
whose extraordinary lives continue to teach the world
about the transforming power of God's Mercy.

aint Mother Teresa of Calcutta
*Whom Jesus asked to bring
His Mercy to the poor*

Canonized September 4, 2016
ionized during the Jubilee Year of Mercy

Saint Faustina Kowalska
*Whom Jesus asked to spread
devotion to His Divine Mercy*

Canonized April 30, 2000
The first saint of the new millennium

This book belongs to:

_____

Mercy is a Way of Loving

What is Love?

Is it just a feeling? Is it just liking someone a lot? That doesn't make sense, because Jesus said, "I say to you, love your enemies." (Matthew 5:44) You see, "love" is not a feeling, **love is something you do: it is doing what you can for the good of another person.** Now this makes sense, right? You can do something for the good of someone that you might not like very much (or someone you don't even know)—and that is love!

Love can change you into a better person, both when you **give love** and when you **receive love**. The Apostle John said, "If we love one another, God abides in us and His love is perfected in us." (1 John 4:12) When we **give** love to others, we also **receive** God's love! And God's love can change you so much that you are not just a better person on earth, but you can become a saint and go to Heaven forever!

So, how do you love others the way God wants you to? Jesus told us the answer: "Be merciful, even as your Father [in Heaven] is merciful." (Luke 6:36) You see, **mercy is a special way of loving: Mercy is doing something good for someone who is suffering.**

"You shall love the Lord your God with all your heart, and with all your soul, and with all your mind, and all your strength." (Mark 12:30)

Love Transforms Our Hearts

What Makes People Suffer?

All suffering is caused by evil in the world, because evil keeps us from having the good that God wants for us. Whenever someone does not have the good that God wants them to have—for their bodies, their minds, or their souls—they suffer.

Jesus came into the world to overcome evil, to go everywhere there is suffering with the merciful love of God. Jesus wants to change everyone in the world with His merciful love. He wants everyone to be more like Him, to love like He loves on earth and to go to Heaven, too!

Can You Love Like Jesus Loves?

You can, by doing the **Works of Mercy**. The Works of Mercy are the **acts of love that Jesus taught us to do** for others who are suffering.

The Works of Mercy overcome evil by giving others the good things they are lacking—for their bodies, their minds, and their souls. And perhaps most important, the kindness you show when you do these works overcomes the loneliness many people feel today.

"Blessed are the merciful, for they shall obtain mercy." (Matthew 5:7)

THE CORPORAL

Works of Mercy

In the Bible, we read from Saint John the Apostle, "If any one says, "I love God," and hates his brother, he is a liar; for he who does not love his brother whom he has seen, cannot love God whom he has not seen." (1 John 4:20)

Read what Jesus says about His Final Judgment when He will send some to Heaven and some to Hell:

"When the Son of Man comes in His glory, and all the angels with Him, then He will sit on His glorious throne. Before Him will be gathered all the nations, and He will separate them one from another as a shepherd separates the sheep from the goats, and He will place the sheep at His right hand, but the goats at the left. Then the King will say to those at His right hand, 'Come, O blessed of My Father, inherit the kingdom prepared for you from the foundation of the world' … Then He will say to those at his left hand, 'Depart from me, you cursed, into the eternal fire prepared for the devil and his angels.'" (Matthew 25:31-34, 41).

How will Jesus separate the sheep from the goats? By how each performed the Corporal Works of Mercy! Jesus said, "Truly, I say to you, as you did [these works of mercy] to one of the least of these My brethren, you did it to Me." (Matthew 25:40)

Saint Mother Teresa called this, "The Gospel on Five Fingers." Just count those last five words of Jesus on each finger: "You did it to Me." She told her sisters, "We cannot do anything for God in Heaven! So what did God do? God became man! Now we can do something for Him, because He said, 'I was hungry and you fed Me! I was thirsty and you gave Me something to drink!'"

The seven Corporal Works of Mercy serve the needs of our bodies. Learn about them in the next pages, then write down your ideas to do them to show your love for God!

Then the righteous will answer Him, 'Lord, when did we see Thee hungry and feed Thee, or thirsty and give Thee drink? And when did we see Thee a stranger and welcome Thee, or naked and clothe Thee? And when did we see Thee sick or in prison and visit Thee?' And the King will answer them, 'Truly, I say to you, as you did it to one of the least of these My brethren, you did it to Me.' (Matthew 25:37-40)

The generous will be blessed, for they share their food with the poor.
(Proverbs 22:9)

How can your family share your food with the poor?
Write down your ideas on the Corporal Works of Mercy page.

First Corporal Work of Mercy
FEED THE HUNGRY

Jesus said to them, "I am the living bread which came down from Heaven;
if any one eats of this bread, he will live for ever; and the bread
which I shall give for the life of the world is My Flesh."
(John 6:51)

Second Corporal Work of Mercy
GIVE DRINK TO THE THIRSTY

"Lord, when did we see Thee…thirsty and give Thee drink?"…And the King will answer them, "Truly, I say to you, as you did it to one of the least of these My brethren, you did it to Me." (Matthew 25:37, 40)

Write down how you can give drink to the thirsty on the Corporal Works of Mercy page.

Saint Mother Teresa of Calcutta said, "We have these words 'I thirst' next to the crucifix in our Missionary of Charity chapels to remind us to quench the thirst of Jesus for souls, for love, for kindness, for compassion…' Until you know deep inside that Jesus thirsts for you—you can't begin to know who He wants to be for you. Or who He wants you to be for Him."

Third Corporal Work of Mercy
CLOTHE THE NAKED

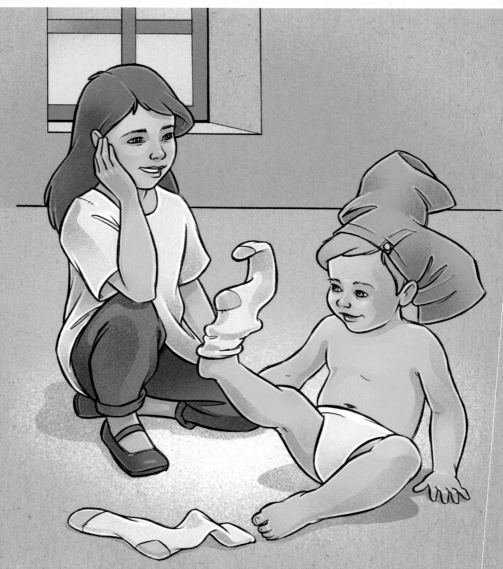

Jesus said, "Whoever has two tunics should share
with the person who has none." (Luke 3:11)

Every person, young and old, needs clothing to protect and respect the gift that
our bodies are. God will resurrect our bodies for Heaven! You can donate, share,
or make clothes for others—what other ways can you clothe the naked?

Third Corporal Work of Mercy
CLOTHE THE NAKED

When Jesus was born, He had no clothes, and when He was crucified, the guards stripped Him of all His clothing before nailing Him to the Cross. "And she gave birth to her first-born son and wrapped Him in swaddling cloths, and laid Him in a manger..." (Luke 2:7) "And they crucified Him, and divided His garments among them, casting lots for them, to decide what each should take." (Mark 15:24)

Not everyone can actually go to a prison, but there are other ways you can show prisoners that Jesus still loves them and thinks of them. You could send rosaries, books, or magazines to prisons, or donate to support people who bring concerts or other beautiful things there. You can also pray like Saint Therese the Little Flower did for a specific prisoner to repent and reconcile with God. Write down your ideas!

Fourth Corporal Work of Mercy
VISIT THE IMPRISONED

When Jesus was arrested, Peter and John followed Him to see what would happen. Peter was scared, so when he was questioned, he denied even knowing Jesus and ran away. But John stayed as close to Jesus as he could—all the way to the foot of the Cross. Think how much this comforted Jesus when He was imprisoned!

Fifth Corporal Work of Mercy
SHELTER THE HOMELESS

We need shelter to protect us from the weather and to give us privacy to feel safe. This is especially important when we are away from our homes.

Think of ideas to help make others feel comfortable and safe, both when they are in their homes and when they are traveling away from home—then write them down on the Corporal Works of Mercy page!

5

Fifth Corporal Work of Mercy
SHELTER THE HOMELESS

The Holy Family had to leave their home in the middle of the night to escape to Egypt from Herod, who was trying to kill Jesus. Think of how grateful they were to everyone who helped them while they traveled without a home!
Jesus said, "Foxes have holes, and birds of the air have nests; but the Son of Man has nowhere to lay His head." (Matthew 8:20)

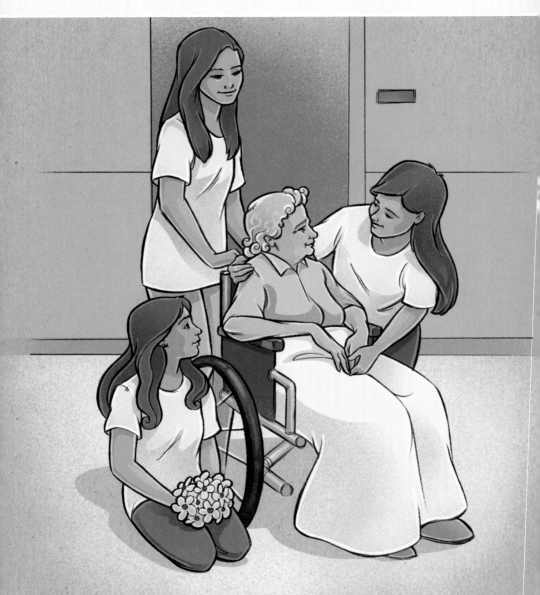

Jesus healed all kinds of sicknesses. Just think: doctors, nurses, and other medical personnel get to take part in this corporal work of mercy for Jesus every day!

We can help the sick and their families, too. What ideas can you think of?

Jesus healed Peter's mother-in-law of a fever and raised the twelve-year-old daughter of Jairus back to life. "And Jesus went about all the cities and villages, teaching in their synagogues and preaching the gospel of the Kingdom, and healing every disease and every infirmity." (Matthew 9:35)

Seventh Corporal Work of Mercy
BURY THE DEAD

Burying the dead shows respect for the sacredness of the bodies God has given us (which will rise again to eternal life) and also helps those who mourn.

Some ways you can perform this work of mercy are by going to a wake, a funeral, or a cemetery. Can you think of other ways to assist people who are suffering the loss of a loved one?

When Jesus was taken down from the Cross, He was laid in the tomb gently by His Blessed Mother, Joseph of Arimathea, Nicodemus, and some other friends. "They took the body of Jesus, and bound it in linen cloths with the spices, as is the burial custom of the Jews. Now in the place where He was crucified there was a garden, and in the garden a new tomb . . . . They laid Jesus there." (John 19:40-42)

THE CORPORAL
Works of Mercy

Here's how I will bring the love of Jesus to people around me ...

_____

_____

_____

_____

_____

_____

_____

_____

_____

_____

MY NOTES, THOUGHTS, AND PRAYERS

_____

_____

_____

_____

_____

_____

_____

_____

_____

_____

_____

_____

_____

THE SPIRITUAL

Works of Mercy

We perform the Corporal Works of Mercy for others just like we are doing them to Jesus. They are done to overcome the evils in the world that deprive people of all the good things God wants for their bodies.

But the Spiritual Works of Mercy are acts of love we do to overcome the greatest of evils, the evil that deprives us of the greatest good there is: the love of God in our hearts and souls. When we accept this love, Jesus does a wonderful thing to us: He makes us more like Himself, transforming us into His brothers and sisters, into sons and daughters of God the Father!

Spiritual evils destroy our friendships with each other and with God. Adam and Eve were friends with God, but by their sin they lost that friendship for all people. Jesus came down from Heaven to restore that friendship. By doing the Spiritual Works of Mercy, we are imitating Jesus, helping others restore their friendship with God in their hearts and souls—and through them Jesus will pour His love into our hearts, too.

Think about how Jesus loves us: even when we reject His love through sin, He keeps offering us His love, His mercy

to overcome the evil of our sins. In the Spiritual Works of Mercy, you will see that Jesus asks us to imitate Him and do these acts of love even if they are not appreciated.

In the Bible, Saint Paul put it this way, "It is no longer I who live, but Christ who lives in me; and the life I now live in the flesh I live by faith in the Son of God, Who loved me and gave Himself for me." (Galatians 2:20)

There are seven Spiritual Works of Mercy. Write down your ideas to do them and help us all become friends of God!

Jesus said, "Who are My brethren?"
And stretching out His hand toward His disciples, He said,
"...For whoever does the Will of My Father in Heaven
is My brother..." (Matthew 12:48-50)

"My brethren, . . . whoever brings back a sinner from the error of his way will save his soul from death and will cover a multitude of sins." (James 5:19-20)

Sin destroys a person's friendship with God—and only God's friends can go to Heaven! Encourage someone to stop sinning and invite them to go to Confession with you—it is like inviting them to go to Heaven! What else could you do?

First Spiritual Work of Mercy
ADMONISH THE SINNER

Jesus said, "If your brother sins, rebuke him; and if he repents, forgive him...there is joy before the angels of God over one sinner who repents." (Luke 17:3, 15:10) "By this we know that we love the children of God, when we love God and obey His commandments. For this is the love of God, that we keep His commandments." (1 John 5:2-3)

Second Spiritual Work of Mercy
INSTRUCT THE IGNORANT

God made our minds to know the truth and to love it. The most important truth is about how to get to Heaven! Because there is evil and sin in the world, our minds often make mistakes and get confused. When you help others know the truth, you are helping them get to Heaven. Jesus said, "I am the Way, and the Truth, and the Life . . . . and you will know the truth, and the truth will make you free." (John 14:6, 8:32). How can you help your friends know the truth about Jesus?

Second Spiritual Work of Mercy
INSTRUCT THE IGNORANT

Jesus said to His Disciples about Heaven, "Enter by the narrow gate ... For the gate is narrow and the way is hard, that leads to life…" (Matthew 7:13-14)

"Jesus had compassion on them, because they were like sheep without a shepherd; and He began to teach them many things." (Mark 6:34)

Third Spiritual Work of Mercy
COUNSEL THE DOUBTFUL

It is easy to get distracted by things in the world today. We can get confused about what God wants us to do, sometimes even doubting what we have been taught by our Catholic Faith. We can be a good friend of God by being a good friend to others, reminding them about God and giving them advice so they keep trying to listen to God and to serve Him—so they can be happy with Him in Heaven!

Third Spiritual Work of Mercy
COUNSEL THE DOUBTFUL

Jesus said, "Peace I leave with you; My peace I give to you. ... Do not let your hearts be troubled or afraid." (John 14:27) A man ran up to Jesus and asked Him, "Good Teacher, what must I do to inherit eternal life?" Jesus said, "You know the commandments." The man replied, "Teacher, all these I have observed from my youth." And Jesus looking upon him loved him . . ." (Mark 10:17-21)

When bad things happen, we get sad. We can be just like Jesus by showing love
to help those who are sad and unhappy. Think of things you can do
to make someone feel better and write them down.

"So humble yourself under the mighty hand of God, that He may exult you in due
time. Cast all your worries upon Him because He cares for you." (1 Peter 5: 6-7)

Fourth Spiritual Work of Mercy
COMFORT THE SORROWFUL

When Jesus' friend Lazarus died, He went to comfort Mary and Martha, the sisters of Lazarus. The Bible says when Jesus saw them weeping, He was deeply moved, and He wept with them. (John 11:33-35)

We know that even people who really love us can make mistakes. Sometimes they blame us for things we didn't do or misunderstand what we say. Other people might not like us, so they do mean things to us. When this happened to Jesus, He showed mercy by not getting angry.

What ideas do you have about how you can imitate Jesus in this way?

Fifth Spiritual Work of Mercy
BEAR WRONGS PATIENTLY

Jesus said, "You have heard that it was said, 'An eye for an eye and a tooth for a tooth.' But I say to you, offer no resistance to one who is evil. When someone strikes you on your right cheek, turn the other one to him as well." (Matt 5:38-39)

Sixth Spiritual Work of Mercy
FORGIVE ALL INJURIES

What do you do when someone tells you they are sorry for something they did? Do you scold them or get angry? Do you tell them, "Never do that again!" That only makes things worse, doesn't it? Remember what you pray in the Our Father: "Forgive us our trespasses, as we forgive those who trespass against us." Show mercy to those who hurt you just like Our Heavenly Father shows mercy to you—by forgiving your sins when you ask Him.

Sixth Spiritual Work of Mercy
FORGIVE ALL INJURIES

When they crucified Him, from the Cross Jesus said, "Father, forgive them,
for they know not what they do." (Luke 23:34)
"Forgiveness demonstrates the presence in the world of the love
which is more powerful than sin." (Pope Saint John Paul II)

Prayers asking God for His Mercy on all people support all the other works of mercy that we can do. As Saint Ignatius of Loyola said, we should, "Pray as if everything depends on God, and work as if everything depended on you."
The Bible tells us that to pray for the dead is a "holy and pious thought ... that they might be delivered from their sin." (2 Maccabees 12:45)
Whom do you want to remember to pray for? Ask others to pray, too!

Jesus prayed to His Father in Heaven for Lazarus, "Father, I thank Thee that Thou hast heard Me. I know that Thou hearest Me always..." Then Jesus cried with a loud voice, "Lazarus, come out." The dead man came out! Jesus said to them, "Unbind him, and let him go." (John 11:38-44)

THE SPIRITUAL
Works of Mercy

Here's how I will bring the love of Jesus to people around me ...

_____

_____

_____

_____

_____

_____

_____

_____

_____

_____

_____

_____

_____

MY NOTES, THOUGHTS, AND PRAYERS

_____

_____

_____

_____

_____

_____

_____

_____

_____

_____

_____

_____

THE TRIBUNAL

of Mercy

Where Jesus said He performs the "Miracle of Divine Mercy"

Jesus appeared many times to Saint Faustina. He gave her several tasks to spread the message of His Divine Mercy to the whole world.

Jesus told Saint Faustina to have a special painting made of Him in a white garment with two rays coming from His Heart and the words, "Jesus, I trust in You" on the bottom. He gave her prayers to pray and to share with the world. He also asked that she convince the Church to institute a new Feast on the Sunday after Easter—Divine Mercy Sunday.

Jesus said to Saint Faustina, **"I am longing to send My Mercy to all souls! Before I come as the Just Judge, I am coming first as the King of Mercy."** What does this mean? That Jesus wants to transform our hearts through His Mercy, so that when He comes to judge our hearts— He will find they have become full of love like His! He will have healed our suffering souls!

This is what Jesus told Saint Faustina:

"Tell souls where they are to look for solace; that is, in the **Tribunal of Mercy. There the greatest miracles take place** [and] are incessantly repeated."

But where is this "Tribunal of Mercy"? Jesus said:

"To avail oneself of this miracle, it is not necessary to go on a great pilgrimage or to carry out some external ceremony; it suffices to come with faith to the feet of My representative [a priest] and to reveal to him one's misery, and the miracle of Divine Mercy will be fully demonstrated. **The miracle of Divine Mercy restores that soul in full.**"

The Tribunal of Mercy is the confessional where you receive from a priest the Sacrament of Penance and Reconciliation when you confess your sins! Go there often so you experience the "miracle of Divine Mercy," too!

THE HOLY MASS

and Mercy

Have you ever noticed how many of the prayers in the Holy Mass beg God for His Mercy?

Why is that? Because **the Mass makes present to us the greatest act of merciful love that has ever occurred**: the offering of the Son of God on the Cross for all of us, to forgive our sins so that God can transform us into His adopted sons and daughters, into brothers and sisters of Christ.

Jesus Himself comes down onto the altar from Heaven during the Holy Mass to feed us with His Body, Blood, Soul, and Divinity in the Eucharist.

Next time you go to Mass, listen and ponder the following prayers (and others) in which we ask for God's mercy:

"Have mercy on us, O Lord. For we have sinned against you. Show us, O Lord, your mercy. And grant us your salvation."

"Lord, have mercy. Christ, have mercy. Lord, have mercy."

"May almighty God have mercy on us, forgive us our sins, and bring us to everlasting life."

"Lord Jesus Christ, Only Begotten Son, Lord God, Lamb of God, Son of the Father, you take away the sins of the world,

have mercy on us; you take away the sins of the world, receive our prayer; you are seated at the right hand of the Father, have mercy on us."

"To you, therefore, most merciful Father, we make humble prayer and petition through Jesus Christ, your Son, our Lord…"

"…in your compassion, O merciful Father, gather to yourself all your children scattered throughout the world…"

"Deliver us, Lord, we pray, from every evil, graciously grant peace in our days, that, by the help of your mercy, we may be always free from sin and safe from all distress, as we await the blessed hope and the coming of our Savior, Jesus Christ."

"Lamb of God, you take away the sins of the world, have mercy on us. Lamb of God, you take away the sins of the world, have mercy on us. Lamb of God, you take away the sins of the world, grant us peace."

THE CHAPLET OF

Divine Mercy

The Divine Mercy Chaplet is a very powerful devotion which was given by Our Lord to Saint Faustina Kowalska. You can pray the Divine Mercy Chaplet with regular rosary beads.

Introductory prayers

After the Sign of the Cross, pray three introductory prayers:
1. The Our Father
2. The Hail, Mary
3. The Apostles' Creed

Prayers for each decade

On the large bead on a rosary before the first decade, say this prayer:

Leader: Eternal Father, I offer you the Body and Blood, Soul and Divinity, of Your dearly beloved Son, Our Lord Jesus Christ,

All: In atonement for our sins and those of the whole world.

On the 10 small beads following each large bead, say this prayer:

Leader: For the sake of His sorrowful Passion,

All: Have mercy on us and on the whole world. *(10 times)*

Continue saying these prayers on the remaining four decades of the rosary.

Closing Prayer
(Say the closing prayer three times)

Holy God, Holy Mighty One,
Holy Immortal One,
have mercy on us and
on the whole world.

Jesus said the
Divine Mercy Chaplet is
especially powerful
when prayed for those
who are dying.

Have FUN learning more about God's Merciful Love!

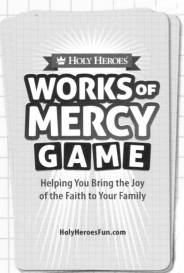

Enjoy the Works of Mercy Game!

This colorful 59-card deck is really "4-games-in-1!"
It contains 28 pairs of illustrated cards showing all the Corporal and Spiritual Works of Mercy ... so kids can see how Jesus' acts of love are connected to theirs.

PLUS ... there are three fun special cards that reinforce ALL the Works of Mercy!

The **Works of Mercy Game** and **game instructions** are available today at

HolyHeroesFun.com

NEW updated Glory Stories® Volume 4 Audio CD!

Glory Stories Volume 4 teaches about the Works of Mercy through the true-life stories of two modern saints!

Saint Mother Teresa of Calcutta
"The Gospel on Five Fingers"—inspires families to live out the Gospel in their own families just as Mother Teresa did on the streets of Calcutta.

Includes a **FREE Bonus Track:** *"What is a Saint?"*

Saint Faustina Kowalska
"Jesus, I Trust in You!"—teaches children about Divine Mercy and the Sacrament of Confession through the life of this saint to whom Jesus appeared numerous times!

Available today at **HolyHeroes.com**

Helping You Bring the Joy of the Faith to Your Family